I'M DOING MY BEST

KNOCK KNOCK® VENICE, CALIFORNIA

Created and published by Knock Knock
Distributed by Who's There Inc.
Venice, CA 90291
knockknockstuff.com

© 2013 Who's There Inc.
All rights reserved
Knock Knock is a trademark of Who's There Inc.
Made in China

ISBN: 978-160106524-7
UPC: 825703-50027-1

20 19 18 17 16 15 14 13 12 11 10 9 8 7 6 5 4 3

YOU WANT
TO BE BETTER

And God knows, you're really trying. So why does it still feel hard? Should it really be *that* tough? Perhaps you were finally going to improve your leadership skills. Or was it a weight loss program? A new fitness regime? No, wait—you were going to stop procrastinating. Get better at guitar?

It doesn't matter how you've decided to improve your life, or how many times you've messed up. What matters is that you're trying. You're really, really trying—even though you secretly want to quit or, at the very least, are already worried about hitting the next wall. That kind of thinking doesn't make you neurotic; it makes you smart and realistic. Anticipating problems is a good thing, despite what some half-baked, pie-in-the-sky types might say. If self-improvement were easy—if there were no obstacles—we'd all be perfect.

You are embarking on a time-honored tradition; people have been trying to improve themselves since the world began. In the 4th Century B.C. the great Greek orator Demosthenes corrected his speech impediment by reciting with stones in his mouth. What are the odds he swallowed a few stones and thought about becoming a shepherd?

Americans, in particular, have a long love affair with self-improvement. It all started with the Puritans, though their efforts at self-improvement may have been more spiritual than ours. ("Become free from sin" vs. "lose ten pounds.") You can see the self-improvement urge in classics like the *Autobiography of Ben Franklin* and George Washington's *Rules of Civility and Decent Behaviour in Company and Conversation*. Self-improvement really got going in the 1930s. Alcoholics Anonymous started in 1935, and the following year, Dale Carnegie published what many consider the first bestselling self-help book, *How to Win Friends and Influence People*. The fifties brought us TV's first big exercise guru, Jack LaLanne; the sixties, Weight Watchers; and the seventies, *The Joy of Sex*.

As long as people have been trying to better themselves, they've faced doubts, setbacks, and failure. While most of us do this anonymously, others have hit road-blocks quite famously. Orville and Wilbur Wright watched a lot of plane crashes before they took off. Twenty-seven publishers turned down Dr. Seuss' first book. Steve Jobs was fired from the company he created. Michael Jordan was cut from his high school basketball team. J. K. Rowling was a broke single mom when she created Harry Potter.

The key to moving beyond setbacks in your quest for self-improvement is resilience. Take stock, correct the problem, learn from it, and keep moving. *Psychology Today* puts it clearly: "There are some common traits among individuals who quickly move past failure and indeed benefit from it. They are able to step back and evaluate their failure. ... They do not become paralyzed by their failed experience."

Whenever you overcome a setback, you'll build confidence that you'll be able to start fresh, again and again, if you need to. Journaling will help you see that progression. If you eat your weight in potato chips or completely lose it at your kids, you can record the lapse, how you responded, and how you moved on.

In addition to helping you keep track of your self-improvement hiccups, journal writing has been shown to have other powerful benefits. As noted self-help guru Deepak Chopra claims, "Journaling is one of the most powerful tools we have to transform our lives," and there is consistent evidence that journal writing aids physical health. According to a widely cited study by James W. Pennebaker and Janel D. Seagal, "Writing about important personal experiences in an emotional way ... brings about improvements in mental and physical health." Proven benefits include better stress management, strengthened immune systems, fewer doctor visits, and improvement in chronic illnesses such as asthma.

It's not entirely clear how journaling accomplishes all this. Catharsis is involved, but many also point to the value of organizing experiences into a cohesive narrative. According to *Newsweek*, some experts believe that journaling "forces us to transform the ruminations cluttering our minds into coherent stories." When you write down each roadblock it becomes a story of how you met the challenge and how you overcame it.

As a devotee of this journal, you obviously have the self-awareness to be honest about your setbacks in the process of trying to reign in whatever needs reigning in, such as that out-of-control spending or plain old bitterness. To take advantage of the journaling process fully, however, don't simply vent about your failures. Instead, record them and then try to understand them.

Specialists agree that in order to reap the benefits of journaling you have to stick with it, quasi-daily, for as little as five minutes at a time (at least fifteen minutes, however, is best). Finding regular writing times and comfortable locations can help with consistency. If you can't think of where to start, use the quotes inside this journal as a jumping-off point for observations and explorations. Finally, determine a home for your journal where you can reference it when the self-improvement journey takes an untoward detour—like near the cookie jar or your credit card.

J. K. Rowling told Harvard's class of 2008, "It is impossible to live without failing at something, unless you live so cautiously that you might as well not have lived at all—in which case, you fail by default. ...The knowledge that you have emerged wiser and stronger from setbacks means that you are, ever after, secure in your ability to survive." Take it from someone who persevered to make millions believe in magic and attempt to play Quidditch: embrace the setbacks, learn from them, and keep on trucking. Or, perhaps just try something else all together.

You may be disappointed if you fail, but you are doomed if you don't try.

BEVERLY SILLS

HOW I'M WORKING ON MYSELF TODAY:

TODAY'S PERSONAL OUTLOOK:

I'd do anything for
a good body except
exercise and eat right.

STEVE MARTIN

HOW I'M WORKING ON MYSELF TODAY:

TODAY'S PERSONAL OUTLOOK:

Real growth often happens outside of where we intend it to, in the interstitial spaces— what Dr. Seuss calls "the waiting place."

BRUCE MAU

DATE		

HOW I'M WORKING ON MYSELF TODAY:

_____

_____

_____

_____

_____

_____

_____

_____

_____

_____

_____

_____

_____

_____

_____

_____

_____

_____

_____

_____

_____

_____

_____

TODAY'S PERSONAL OUTLOOK:

In any case you mustn't confuse a single failure with a final defeat.

F. SCOTT FITZGERALD

DATE		

HOW I'M WORKING ON MYSELF TODAY:

_____

_____

_____

_____

_____

_____

_____

_____

_____

_____

_____

_____

_____

_____

_____

_____

_____

_____

_____

_____

_____

TODAY'S PERSONAL OUTLOOK:

Even though you get the monkey off your back, the circus never really leaves town.

ANNE LAMOTT

HOW I'M WORKING ON MYSELF TODAY:

_____

_____

_____

_____

_____

_____

_____

_____

_____

_____

_____

_____

_____

_____

_____

_____

_____

_____

_____

_____

_____

_____

_____

TODAY'S PERSONAL OUTLOOK:

The brick walls are there for a reason. They're not there to keep us out. The brick walls are there to give us a chance to show how badly we want something.

RANDY PAUSCH

DATE		

HOW I'M WORKING ON MYSELF TODAY:

_____

_____

_____

_____

_____

_____

_____

_____

_____

_____

_____

_____

_____

_____

_____

_____

_____

_____

_____

_____

_____

_____

_____

_____

_____

TODAY'S PERSONAL OUTLOOK:

If I had to live my life again, I'd make all the same mistakes, only sooner.

TALLULAH BANKHEAD

	DATE	

HOW I'M WORKING ON MYSELF TODAY:

_____

_____

_____

_____

_____

_____

_____

_____

_____

_____

_____

_____

_____

_____

_____

_____

_____

_____

_____

_____

_____

_____

TODAY'S PERSONAL OUTLOOK:

She would be a new person, she vowed.
They said no matter how far a mule
travels it can never come back a horse,
but she would show them all.

JUNOT DÍAZ

HOW I'M WORKING ON MYSELF TODAY:

_____

_____

_____

_____

_____

_____

_____

_____

_____

_____

_____

_____

_____

_____

_____

_____

_____

_____

_____

_____

_____

_____

_____

_____

_____

TODAY'S PERSONAL OUTLOOK:

I really don't think I need buns of steel. I'd be happy with buns of cinnamon.

ELLEN DEGENERES

	DATE	

HOW I'M WORKING ON MYSELF TODAY:

_____

_____

_____

_____

_____

_____

_____

_____

_____

_____

_____

_____

_____

_____

_____

_____

_____

_____

_____

_____

_____

_____

_____

_____

TODAY'S PERSONAL OUTLOOK:

It's a good thing to have all the props pulled out from under us occasionally. It gives us some sense of what is rock under our feet, and what is sand.

MADELEINE L'ENGLE

	DATE	

HOW I'M WORKING ON MYSELF TODAY:

_____

_____

_____

_____

_____

_____

_____

_____

_____

_____

_____

_____

_____

_____

_____

_____

_____

_____

_____

_____

_____

_____

TODAY'S PERSONAL OUTLOOK:

There's only one corner of the universe you can be certain of improving, and that's your own self.

———————

ALDOUS HUXLEY

HOW I'M WORKING ON MYSELF TODAY:

TODAY'S PERSONAL OUTLOOK:

Every day is a new beginning and a chance to blow it.

CATHY GUISEWITE

DATE		

HOW I'M WORKING ON MYSELF TODAY:

_____

_____

_____

_____

_____

_____

_____

_____

_____

_____

_____

_____

_____

_____

_____

_____

_____

_____

_____

_____

_____

_____

_____

TODAY'S PERSONAL OUTLOOK:

You can't turn a sow's ear into veal Orloff, but you can do something very good with a sow's ear.

JULIA CHILD

DATE		

HOW I'M WORKING ON MYSELF TODAY:

_____

_____

_____

_____

_____

_____

_____

_____

_____

_____

_____

_____

_____

_____

_____

_____

_____

_____

_____

_____

_____

_____

_____

_____

TODAY'S PERSONAL OUTLOOK:

I suppose it is tempting, if the only tool you have is a hammer, to treat everything as if it were a nail.

ABRAHAM MASLOW

DATE		

HOW I'M WORKING ON MYSELF TODAY:

_____

_____

_____

_____

_____

_____

_____

_____

_____

_____

_____

_____

_____

_____

_____

_____

_____

_____

_____

_____

_____

_____

_____

_____

_____

_____

TODAY'S PERSONAL OUTLOOK:

Woe-is-me is not an attractive narrative.

MAUREEN DOWD

DATE		

HOW I'M WORKING ON MYSELF TODAY:

_____

_____

_____

_____

_____

_____

_____

_____

_____

_____

_____

_____

_____

_____

_____

_____

_____

_____

_____

_____

_____

_____

_____

_____

_____

_____

TODAY'S PERSONAL OUTLOOK:

It is a common experience that a problem difficult at night is resolved in the morning after the committee of sleep has worked on it.

——————

JOHN STEINBECK

DATE		

HOW I'M WORKING ON MYSELF TODAY:

_____

_____

_____

_____

_____

_____

_____

_____

_____

_____

_____

_____

_____

_____

_____

_____

_____

_____

_____

_____

_____

_____

_____

_____

_____

_____

TODAY'S PERSONAL OUTLOOK:

The need for change
bulldozed a road down
the center of my mind.

MAYA ANGELOU

	DATE	

HOW I'M WORKING ON MYSELF TODAY:

_____

_____

_____

_____

_____

_____

_____

_____

_____

_____

_____

_____

_____

_____

_____

_____

_____

_____

_____

_____

_____

_____

_____

_____

TODAY'S PERSONAL OUTLOOK:

A quilt may take a year, but if you just keep doing it, you get a quilt.

CHUCK CLOSE

HOW I'M WORKING ON MYSELF TODAY:

_____

_____

_____

_____

_____

_____

_____

_____

_____

_____

_____

_____

_____

_____

_____

_____

_____

_____

_____

_____

TODAY'S PERSONAL OUTLOOK:

All life is an experiment. . . .
What if you do fail, and get fairly
rolled in the dirt once or twice?
Up again, you shall never be so
afraid of a tumble.

RALPH WALDO EMERSON

DATE		

HOW I'M WORKING ON MYSELF TODAY:

_____

_____

_____

_____

_____

_____

_____

_____

_____

_____

_____

_____

_____

_____

_____

_____

_____

_____

_____

_____

_____

_____

_____

TODAY'S PERSONAL OUTLOOK:

Diets are not there to be picked and mixed but picked and stuck to, which is exactly what I shall begin to do once I've eaten this chocolate croissant.

HELEN FIELDING

DATE		

HOW I'M WORKING ON MYSELF TODAY:

_____

_____

_____

_____

_____

_____

_____

_____

_____

_____

_____

_____

_____

_____

_____

_____

_____

_____

_____

_____

_____

_____

TODAY'S PERSONAL OUTLOOK:

If you want to slip into a round hole, you must make a ball of yourself.

GEORGE ELIOT

HOW I'M WORKING ON MYSELF TODAY:

_____

_____

_____

_____

_____

_____

_____

_____

_____

_____

_____

_____

_____

_____

_____

_____

_____

_____

_____

_____

_____

_____

_____

TODAY'S PERSONAL OUTLOOK:

Whenever I go on a ride, I'm always thinking of what's wrong with the thing and how it can be improved.

———

WALT DISNEY

DATE		

HOW I'M WORKING ON MYSELF TODAY:

_____

_____

_____

_____

_____

_____

_____

_____

_____

_____

_____

_____

_____

_____

_____

_____

_____

_____

_____

_____

_____

_____

_____

_____

_____

_____

_____

TODAY'S PERSONAL OUTLOOK:

A problem is a chance for you to do your best.

DUKE ELLINGTON

DATE		

HOW I'M WORKING ON MYSELF TODAY:

_____

_____

_____

_____

_____

_____

_____

_____

_____

_____

_____

_____

_____

_____

_____

_____

_____

_____

_____

_____

_____

_____

_____

_____

_____

TODAY'S PERSONAL OUTLOOK:

Ever tried. Ever failed. No matter. Try again. Fail again. Fail better.

SAMUEL BECKETT

HOW I'M WORKING ON MYSELF TODAY:

_____

_____

_____

_____

_____

_____

_____

_____

_____

_____

_____

_____

_____

_____

_____

_____

_____

_____

_____

_____

_____

_____

_____

_____

_____

TODAY'S PERSONAL OUTLOOK:

The slogan "press on" has solved and always will solve the problems of the human race.

CALVIN COOLIDGE

DATE		

HOW I'M WORKING ON MYSELF TODAY:

_____

_____

_____

_____

_____

_____

_____

_____

_____

_____

_____

_____

_____

_____

_____

_____

_____

_____

_____

_____

_____

_____

_____

_____

_____

_____

TODAY'S PERSONAL OUTLOOK:

The problem with self-improvement is knowing when to quit.

DAVID LEE ROTH

HOW I'M WORKING ON MYSELF TODAY:

_____

_____

_____

_____

_____

_____

_____

_____

_____

_____

_____

_____

_____

_____

_____

_____

_____

_____

_____

_____

_____

_____

_____

_____

TODAY'S PERSONAL OUTLOOK:

Talent is insignificant. I know a lot of talented ruins. Beyond talent lie all the usual words: discipline, love, luck, but, most of all, endurance.

JAMES BALDWIN

HOW I'M WORKING ON MYSELF TODAY:

_____

_____

_____

_____

_____

_____

_____

_____

_____

_____

_____

_____

_____

_____

_____

_____

_____

_____

_____

_____

_____

_____

_____

TODAY'S PERSONAL OUTLOOK:

I think I'm the happiest I've ever been. Part of it is just learning what makes me happier and doing more of it, and learning what makes me unhappier and doing less of it.

MARK FRAUENFELDER

DATE		

HOW I'M WORKING ON MYSELF TODAY:

_____

_____

_____

_____

_____

_____

_____

_____

_____

_____

_____

_____

_____

_____

_____

_____

_____

_____

_____

_____

_____

_____

_____

_____

TODAY'S PERSONAL OUTLOOK:

When all else fails, you always have delusion.

CONAN O'BRIEN

DATE

HOW I'M WORKING ON MYSELF TODAY:

_____

_____

_____

_____

_____

_____

_____

_____

_____

_____

_____

_____

_____

_____

_____

_____

_____

_____

_____

_____

_____

_____

_____

_____

_____

_____

_____

TODAY'S PERSONAL OUTLOOK:

You can't be that kid standing at the top of the waterslide, overthinking it. You have to go down the chute.

TINA FEY

DATE		

HOW I'M WORKING ON MYSELF TODAY:

_____

_____

_____

_____

_____

_____

_____

_____

_____

_____

_____

_____

_____

_____

_____

_____

_____

_____

_____

_____

_____

_____

_____

_____

_____

_____

TODAY'S PERSONAL OUTLOOK:

It's our choices, Harry, that show what we truly are, far more than our abilities.

J. K. ROWLING

HOW I'M WORKING ON MYSELF TODAY:

_____

_____

_____

_____

_____

_____

_____

_____

_____

_____

_____

_____

_____

_____

_____

_____

_____

_____

_____

_____

_____

_____

_____

_____

_____

_____

_____

_____

_____

_____

TODAY'S PERSONAL OUTLOOK:

When you reach for the stars, you may not quite get them, but you won't come up with a handful of mud either.

LEO BURNETT

HOW I'M WORKING ON MYSELF TODAY:

_____

_____

_____

_____

_____

_____

_____

_____

_____

_____

_____

_____

_____

_____

_____

_____

_____

_____

_____

_____

_____

_____

_____

TODAY'S PERSONAL OUTLOOK:

Every new adjustment is a crisis in self-esteem.

ERIC HOFFER

	DATE	

HOW I'M WORKING ON MYSELF TODAY:

_____

_____

_____

_____

_____

_____

_____

_____

_____

_____

_____

_____

_____

_____

_____

_____

_____

_____

_____

_____

_____

_____

_____

_____

TODAY'S PERSONAL OUTLOOK:

I think somehow
we learn who we
really are and then
live with that decision.

ELEANOR ROOSEVELT

DATE		

HOW I'M WORKING ON MYSELF TODAY:

_____

_____

_____

_____

_____

_____

_____

_____

_____

_____

_____

_____

_____

_____

_____

_____

_____

_____

_____

_____

_____

_____

_____

_____

TODAY'S PERSONAL OUTLOOK:

Everybody has talent, and it's just a matter of moving around until you've discovered what it is.

GEORGE LUCAS

DATE		

HOW I'M WORKING ON MYSELF TODAY:

_____

_____

_____

_____

_____

_____

_____

_____

_____

_____

_____

_____

_____

_____

_____

_____

_____

_____

_____

_____

_____

_____

_____

_____

_____

TODAY'S PERSONAL OUTLOOK:

The moment of change is the only poem.

ADRIENNE RICH

DATE		

HOW I'M WORKING ON MYSELF TODAY:

_____

_____

_____

_____

_____

_____

_____

_____

_____

_____

_____

_____

_____

_____

_____

_____

_____

_____

_____

_____

_____

_____

_____

_____

TODAY'S PERSONAL OUTLOOK:

Sometimes I lie awake at night, and I ask, "Where have I gone wrong?" Then a voice says to me, "This is going to take more than one night."

CHARLES M. SCHULZ

DATE

HOW I'M WORKING ON MYSELF TODAY:

_____

_____

_____

_____

_____

_____

_____

_____

_____

_____

_____

_____

_____

_____

_____

_____

_____

_____

_____

_____

_____

_____

_____

_____

_____

_____

_____

TODAY'S PERSONAL OUTLOOK:

In the middle of the winter I learned at last that there was in me an invincible summer.

ALBERT CAMUS

HOW I'M WORKING ON MYSELF TODAY:

_____

_____

_____

_____

_____

_____

_____

_____

_____

_____

_____

_____

_____

_____

_____

_____

_____

_____

_____

_____

_____

_____

_____

_____

_____

TODAY'S PERSONAL OUTLOOK:

Man is a nerve of the cosmos, dislocated, trying to quiver into place.

JEAN TOOMER

DATE		

HOW I'M WORKING ON MYSELF TODAY:

_____

_____

_____

_____

_____

_____

_____

_____

_____

_____

_____

_____

_____

_____

_____

_____

_____

_____

_____

_____

_____

_____

_____

_____

_____

_____

_____

_____

TODAY'S PERSONAL OUTLOOK:

Hope and change are hard-fought things.

MICHELLE OBAMA

HOW I'M WORKING ON MYSELF TODAY:

_____

_____

_____

_____

_____

_____

_____

_____

_____

_____

_____

_____

_____

_____

_____

_____

_____

_____

_____

_____

_____

_____

_____

_____

_____

_____

_____

_____

TODAY'S PERSONAL OUTLOOK:

My happiness grows in direct proportion to my acceptance and in inverse proportion to my expectations.

MICHAEL J. FOX

DATE		

HOW I'M WORKING ON MYSELF TODAY:

_____

_____

_____

_____

_____

_____

_____

_____

_____

_____

_____

_____

_____

_____

_____

_____

_____

_____

_____

_____

_____

_____

_____

_____

_____

_____

TODAY'S PERSONAL OUTLOOK:

I think that anyone who's pushed to do the very best that they can is privileged. It's a luxury.

TWYLA THARP

HOW I'M WORKING ON MYSELF TODAY:

_____

_____

_____

_____

_____

_____

_____

_____

_____

_____

_____

_____

_____

_____

_____

_____

_____

_____

_____

_____

_____

_____

_____

_____

TODAY'S PERSONAL OUTLOOK:

And the trouble is, if you don't risk anything, you risk even *more*.

ERICA JONG

DATE		

HOW I'M WORKING ON MYSELF TODAY:

Sometimes people let the same problem make them miserable for years when they could just say, "So what." That's one of my favorite things to say. "So what."

ANDY WARHOL

DATE		

HOW I'M WORKING ON MYSELF TODAY:

_____

_____

_____

_____

_____

_____

_____

_____

_____

_____

_____

_____

_____

_____

_____

_____

_____

_____

_____

_____

_____

_____

_____

_____

TODAY'S PERSONAL OUTLOOK:

The indispensable first step to getting the things you want out of life is this: Decide what you want.

———

BEN STEIN

DATE		

HOW I'M WORKING ON MYSELF TODAY:

_____

_____

_____

_____

_____

_____

_____

_____

_____

_____

_____

_____

_____

_____

_____

_____

_____

_____

_____

_____

_____

_____

_____

_____

_____

_____

_____

_____

_____

_____

TODAY'S PERSONAL OUTLOOK:

Abstainer. A weak man who yields to the temptation of denying himself a pleasure.

AMBROSE BIERCE

DATE		

HOW I'M WORKING ON MYSELF TODAY:

_____

_____

_____

_____

_____

_____

_____

_____

_____

_____

_____

_____

_____

_____

_____

_____

_____

_____

_____

_____

_____

_____

TODAY'S PERSONAL OUTLOOK:

One setback is
one setback—
it is not the
end of the world.

JILLIAN MICHAELS

DATE		

HOW I'M WORKING ON MYSELF TODAY:

_____

_____

_____

_____

_____

_____

_____

_____

_____

_____

_____

_____

_____

_____

_____

_____

_____

_____

_____

_____

_____

_____

_____

_____

_____

_____

TODAY'S PERSONAL OUTLOOK:

The only thing
that I have done
that is not mitigated
by luck, diminished
by good fortune,
is that I persisted.
And other people
gave up.

HARRISON FORD

DATE		

HOW I'M WORKING ON MYSELF TODAY:

_____

_____

_____

_____

_____

_____

_____

_____

_____

_____

_____

_____

_____

_____

_____

_____

_____

_____

_____

_____

_____

_____

_____

_____

_____

_____

_____

TODAY'S PERSONAL OUTLOOK:

By not trying we throw away the chance of an immense good; by not succeeding we only incur the loss of a little human labor.

FRANCIS BACON

DATE		

HOW I'M WORKING ON MYSELF TODAY:

_____

_____

_____

_____

_____

_____

_____

_____

_____

_____

_____

_____

_____

_____

_____

_____

_____

_____

_____

_____

_____

_____

_____

_____

_____

TODAY'S PERSONAL OUTLOOK:

A sobering thought: What if, at this very moment, I am living up to my full potential?

JANE WAGNER

DATE		

HOW I'M WORKING ON MYSELF TODAY:

_____

_____

_____

_____

_____

_____

_____

_____

_____

_____

_____

_____

_____

_____

_____

_____

_____

_____

_____

_____

_____

_____

_____

_____

TODAY'S PERSONAL OUTLOOK:

Like a fish which swims calmly
in deep water, I felt all about me
the secure supporting pressure of
my own life. Ragged, inglorious, and
apparently purposeless, but my own.

IRIS MURDOCH

DATE		

HOW I'M WORKING ON MYSELF TODAY:

_____

_____

_____

_____

_____

_____

_____

_____

_____

_____

_____

_____

_____

_____

_____

_____

_____

_____

_____

_____

_____

_____

_____

_____

_____

_____

TODAY'S PERSONAL OUTLOOK:

We choose to go to the moon in this decade and do the other things, not because they are easy, but because they are hard.

JOHN F. KENNEDY

DATE		

HOW I'M WORKING ON MYSELF TODAY:

_____

_____

_____

_____

_____

_____

_____

_____

_____

_____

_____

_____

_____

_____

_____

_____

_____

_____

_____

_____

_____

_____

_____

TODAY'S PERSONAL OUTLOOK:

As one gets older . . . one discovers that everything is always going to be exactly the same with different hats on.

NOËL COWARD

HOW I'M WORKING ON MYSELF TODAY:

_____

_____

_____

_____

_____

_____

_____

_____

_____

_____

_____

_____

_____

_____

_____

_____

_____

_____

_____

_____

_____

_____

TODAY'S PERSONAL OUTLOOK:

You can settle for
reality, or you can
go off, like a fool, and
dream another dream.

NORA EPHRON

DATE		

HOW I'M WORKING ON MYSELF TODAY:

_____

_____

_____

_____

_____

_____

_____

_____

_____

_____

_____

_____

_____

_____

_____

_____

_____

_____

_____

_____

_____

_____

_____

_____

_____

_____

_____

TODAY'S PERSONAL OUTLOOK:

Blame someone else and get on with your life.

ALAN WOODS

DATE		

HOW I'M WORKING ON MYSELF TODAY:

_____

_____

_____

_____

_____

_____

_____

_____

_____

_____

_____

_____

_____

_____

_____

_____

_____

_____

_____

_____

_____

_____

_____

_____

_____

_____

_____

TODAY'S PERSONAL OUTLOOK:

People wish to learn to swim and at the same time to keep one foot on the ground.

MARCEL PROUST

HOW I'M WORKING ON MYSELF TODAY:

_____

_____

_____

_____

_____

_____

_____

_____

_____

_____

_____

_____

_____

_____

_____

_____

_____

_____

_____

_____

_____

_____

_____

_____

_____

_____

_____

_____

_____

_____

_____

TODAY'S PERSONAL OUTLOOK:

When asked,
"How do you write?"
I invariably answer,
"One word at a time."

STEPHEN KING

DATE		

HOW I'M WORKING ON MYSELF TODAY:

_____

_____

_____

_____

_____

_____

_____

_____

_____

_____

_____

_____

_____

_____

_____

_____

_____

_____

_____

_____

_____

_____

_____

_____

_____

_____

TODAY'S PERSONAL OUTLOOK:

Habit is overcome by habit.

DESIDERIUS ERASMUS

DATE		

HOW I'M WORKING ON MYSELF TODAY:

_____

_____

_____

_____

_____

_____

_____

_____

_____

_____

_____

_____

_____

_____

_____

_____

_____

_____

_____

_____

_____

_____

_____

_____

_____

_____

_____

_____

_____

_____

TODAY'S PERSONAL OUTLOOK:

Failure is not our only punishment for laziness; there is also the success of others.

JULES RENARD

DATE		

HOW I'M WORKING ON MYSELF TODAY:

_____
_____
_____
_____
_____
_____
_____
_____
_____
_____
_____
_____
_____
_____
_____
_____
_____
_____
_____
_____
_____
_____
_____
_____
_____
_____
_____
_____
_____
_____
_____
_____

TODAY'S PERSONAL OUTLOOK:

When we lose twenty pounds, . . . we may be losing the twenty best pounds we have! We may be losing the pounds that contain our genius, our humanity, our love and honesty.

WOODY ALLEN

DATE		

HOW I'M WORKING ON MYSELF TODAY:

_____

_____

_____

_____

_____

_____

_____

_____

_____

_____

_____

_____

_____

_____

_____

_____

_____

_____

_____

_____

_____

_____

_____

TODAY'S PERSONAL OUTLOOK:

Like anyone else,
she must have wanted
different things at the
same time. The human
heart is a dark forest.

TOBIAS WOLFF

DATE		

HOW I'M WORKING ON MYSELF TODAY:

_____

_____

_____

_____

_____

_____

_____

_____

_____

_____

_____

_____

_____

_____

_____

_____

_____

_____

_____

_____

_____

_____

_____

TODAY'S PERSONAL OUTLOOK:

The triumph of anything is a matter of organization. If there are such things as angels, I hope that they are organized along the lines of the Mafia.

KURT VONNEGUT

HOW I'M WORKING ON MYSELF TODAY:

_____

_____

_____

_____

_____

_____

_____

_____

_____

_____

_____

_____

_____

_____

_____

_____

_____

_____

_____

_____

_____

_____

TODAY'S PERSONAL OUTLOOK:

Achieving a goal is nothing. The getting there is everything.

JULES MICHELET

DATE		

HOW I'M WORKING ON MYSELF TODAY:

_____

_____

_____

_____

_____

_____

_____

_____

_____

_____

_____

_____

_____

_____

_____

_____

_____

_____

_____

_____

_____

_____

_____

_____

_____

_____

_____

TODAY'S PERSONAL OUTLOOK:

Discipline should not be practiced like a
rule imposed on oneself from the outside,
but that it becomes an expression of one's
own will; that it is felt as pleasant, and that
one slowly accustoms oneself to a kind of
behavior which one would eventually miss,
if one stopped practicing it.

ERICH FROMM

DATE		

HOW I'M WORKING ON MYSELF TODAY:

_____

_____

_____

_____

_____

_____

_____

_____

_____

_____

_____

_____

_____

_____

_____

_____

_____

_____

_____

_____

_____

_____

_____

_____

_____

_____

_____

_____

_____

_____

_____

_____

TODAY'S PERSONAL OUTLOOK:

If you don't place your foot on the rope, you'll never cross the chasm.

LIZ SMITH

HOW I'M WORKING ON MYSELF TODAY:

_____

_____

_____

_____

_____

_____

_____

_____

_____

_____

_____

_____

_____

_____

_____

_____

_____

_____

_____

_____

_____

_____

_____

_____

TODAY'S PERSONAL OUTLOOK:

Birthday resolution: From now on specialize; never again make any concession to the ninety-nine parts of you which are like everybody else at the expense of the one which is unique.

CYRIL CONNOLLY

	DATE	

HOW I'M WORKING ON MYSELF TODAY:

_____

_____

_____

_____

_____

_____

_____

_____

_____

_____

_____

_____

_____

_____

_____

_____

_____

_____

_____

_____

_____

_____

_____

_____

_____

_____

_____

TODAY'S PERSONAL OUTLOOK:

Poor me. There's nothing so sweet
as wallowing in it is there? Wallowing
is sex for depressives.

JEANETTE WINTERSON

DATE		

HOW I'M WORKING ON MYSELF TODAY:

_____

_____

_____

_____

_____

_____

_____

_____

_____

_____

_____

_____

_____

_____

_____

_____

_____

_____

_____

_____

_____

_____

_____

_____

TODAY'S PERSONAL OUTLOOK:

Anyone can have an off decade.

LARRY COLE

DATE		

HOW I'M WORKING ON MYSELF TODAY:

_____

_____

_____

_____

_____

_____

_____

_____

_____

_____

_____

_____

_____

_____

_____

_____

_____

_____

_____

_____

_____

_____

_____

_____

_____

_____

_____

_____

TODAY'S PERSONAL OUTLOOK:

Clinging to the past is the problem. Embracing change is the solution.

GLORIA STEINEM

DATE

HOW I'M WORKING ON MYSELF TODAY:

_____

_____

_____

_____

_____

_____

_____

_____

_____

_____

_____

_____

_____

_____

_____

_____

_____

_____

_____

_____

_____

_____

_____

TODAY'S PERSONAL OUTLOOK:

Experience is the name everyone gives to their mistakes.

OSCAR WILDE

DATE		

HOW I'M WORKING ON MYSELF TODAY:

_____

_____

_____

_____

_____

_____

_____

_____

_____

_____

_____

_____

_____

_____

_____

_____

_____

_____

_____

_____

_____

_____

_____

TODAY'S PERSONAL OUTLOOK:

One must have chaos within to enable one to give birth to a dancing star.

FRIEDRICH NIETZSCHE

DATE		

HOW I'M WORKING ON MYSELF TODAY:

_____

_____

_____

_____

_____

_____

_____

_____

_____

_____

_____

_____

_____

_____

_____

_____

_____

_____

_____

_____

_____

_____

_____

_____

_____

TODAY'S PERSONAL OUTLOOK:

I do the very best
I know how—the very
best I can; and I mean
to keep on doing so until
the end.

———————————

ABRAHAM LINCOLN

HOW I'M WORKING ON MYSELF TODAY:

_____

_____

_____

_____

_____

_____

_____

_____

_____

_____

_____

_____

_____

_____

_____

_____

_____

_____

_____

_____

_____

_____

_____

_____

_____

_____

_____

_____

TODAY'S PERSONAL OUTLOOK:

I made no resolutions for the New Year. The habit of making plans, of criticizing, sanctioning and molding my life, is too much of a daily event for me.

———

ANAÏS NIN

	DATE	

HOW I'M WORKING ON MYSELF TODAY:

_____

_____

_____

_____

_____

_____

_____

_____

_____

_____

_____

_____

_____

_____

_____

_____

_____

_____

_____

_____

_____

_____

_____

_____

_____

_____

TODAY'S PERSONAL OUTLOOK:

Knowing what you cannot do is more important than knowing what you can do. In fact, that's good taste.

LUCILLE BALL

DATE		

HOW I'M WORKING ON MYSELF TODAY:

_____

_____

_____

_____

_____

_____

_____

_____

_____

_____

_____

_____

_____

_____

_____

_____

_____

_____

_____

_____

_____

_____

_____

_____

_____

_____

_____

_____

_____

_____

_____

TODAY'S PERSONAL OUTLOOK:

Let us cultivate our garden.

VOLTAIRE

DATE		

HOW I'M WORKING ON MYSELF TODAY:

_____

_____

_____

_____

_____

_____

_____

_____

_____

_____

_____

_____

_____

_____

_____

_____

_____

_____

_____

_____

_____

_____

_____

_____

_____

_____

_____

_____

_____

TODAY'S PERSONAL OUTLOOK:

She hoped to be wise
and reasonable in time;
but alas! alas! she must
confess to herself that
she was not wise yet.

JANE AUSTEN

HOW I'M WORKING ON MYSELF TODAY:

_____

_____

_____

_____

_____

_____

_____

_____

_____

_____

_____

_____

_____

_____

_____

_____

_____

_____

_____

_____

_____

_____

_____

TODAY'S PERSONAL OUTLOOK:

After all, tomorrow is another day.

MARGARET MITCHELL

DATE		

HOW I'M WORKING ON MYSELF TODAY:

_____

_____

_____

_____

_____

_____

_____

_____

_____

_____

_____

_____

_____

_____

_____

_____

_____

_____

_____

_____

_____

_____

TODAY'S PERSONAL OUTLOOK:

Keep your chin up.

———————

KNOCK KNOCK